Previous pages: Mounted officer and police transport wagon, probably somewhere in lower Manhattan, circa 1912.

Mounted policeman with flag, from Spring 3100.

Howard Chandler Christy
June 1925

N.Y.P.D.: AN ILLUSTRATED HISTORY

CLOSE-UP FEATURES

COLONIAL POLICING

In 1625, employees of the Dutch West India Company became the first Europeans to settle in what is now Manhattan. Peter Minuit, the leader of the expedition, purchased the island from the Munsee Indians and appointed Jan (or Johann) Lampo as the trading post's "schout-fiscal," or "sheriff-prosecutor," thus beginning the long history of policing in New York City.

The residents of New Amsterdam, the tiny settlement at Manhattan's southern tip, were mostly Dutch fur traders, farmers, and craftsmen. A few dissolute apprentices who liked to drink on the Sabbath were the only threat to law and order, and despite their occasional brawls, the schout's duties were light. Between 1626 and 1631, only two crimes rose to the level of a whipping, the preferred method of punishment in a community without a jail.

In 1638, New Amsterdam experienced what may be termed its first crime wave. The population was now around 400 souls, only a narrow majority of them Dutch. The rest were from England, France, Germany, and Ireland; most were male and employed as household servants, soldiers, or apprentices. Runaway servants from the nearby English colonies swelled this restless and foreign underclass, and Dutch leaders considered them generally unruly and rebellious. In May 1638, a soldier named Gerrit Jansen was stabbed to death in front of Fort Amsterdam, becoming New York's first murder victim. In response, the colony's directors passed the earliest city ordinances against intoxication and harboring sailors, who were prone to carousing on shore leave. Crime, usually inflamed by alcohol, nevertheless increased, and New Amsterdam earned a reputation as one of the most boisterous towns in North America.

Above: A wooden rattle carried by members of the Dutch Rattle-watch, 1651. Rattles were used to alert colonists in the event of fire or other danger in the night.

Left: The Rattle-watch prepares to patrol from sunset until dawn.

Opposite: A ceramic pitcher, late nineteenth century, depicting a Rattle-watchman of New Amsterdam on his rounds with pike and lantern.

Above: Bellmen going their rounds, circa 1750.

Below: Man in the stocks, seventeenth century.

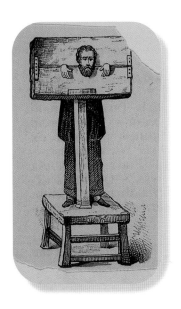

By the 1650s, more than a quarter of the city buildings had been converted into brandy shops or beer houses. Even Peter Stuyvesant, the West India Company's law-and-order director-general, had failed to stem the rise of drunkenness. In 1658, the burgomasters voted to establish an eight-man Rattle-watch to patrol New Amsterdam's narrow and muddy streets from nine until dawn.

Modeled after the nighttime watches that guarded most Western European cities, the watchmen were supposed to walk the streets with a lantern to light their way and call out the hour on every corner. If they saw a fire—a constant danger in the closely built town—they used their loud wooden rattles to wake the neighbors, who immediately formed a bucket brigade. Anyone found "disturbing the peace or lurking about any person's house or committing any theft" was captured and held until the schout woke the following morning. Led by Captain Lodowyck Pos, the eight men of the Rattle-watch were New York's first police force.

The Watch, as it was known, acted as the City's primary police force for the next 180 years. In 1664, the British ejected the Dutch and divided New York City into six wards. The citizens elected a constable for each ward whose main duty was to make sure the taverns were shut and drunkards were kept off the streets during the Sunday services. At night, a watch made up of "good and honest Inhabitants householders" patrolled the wards and called out the hours. Similar systems of constable and night-time watchmen were instituted in the neighboring counties of Brooklyn, Queens, Staten Island, and the Bronx, then rural farming communities.

Though most New Yorkers deemed the watch necessary, they frequently argued about how to organize it. During some eras the City hired paid patrols, though the additional taxes were unpopular and the salary was so low that the authorities had a hard time finding recruits. When their frustrations at the paid watch became too great, the citizens decided to share the responsibility for patrolling the City among themselves. This caused difficulties for the poor, who still had to work days while the rich could hire replacements to take their patrols. The substitutes were often disreputable and lazy; a newspaper called them a "Parcel of idle, drinking, vigilant Snorers, who never quell'd any nocturnal Tumult in their Lives." Due to these problems, the number of watchmen rose slowly relative to the population, and the crime rate increased despite ever harsher punishments.

Early eighteenth-century New York City was not a safe place to live. At night, the streets were dark, and citizens traveled in twos or threes to lessen their chances of being mugged. Constables were frequently attacked by indignant criminals when trying to make arrests.

Above: Stocks from the Dutch days, circa 1660s.

Below: (top) A folding knife that can also fire a bullet, circa 1885. (bottom) A single-shot flintlock pistol, circa 1790. These weapons are typical of those that would have been confiscated by police officers.

Portrait of Jacob Hays, High Constable of New York (1801–1844)

THE BIRTH OF A PROFESSIONAL FORCE

After the defeat of the British in 1783, the crime wave abated somewhat despite New York's population growth from 33,000 in 1790 to 123,000 in 1820. Law enforcement was overseen by the High Constable, who had to fight both crime and efforts by the City government to cut back the personnel in his squad. More than a century of British rule had given the citizenry a deep antiauthoritarian streak, and people were suspicious of any efforts to establish what they saw as another standing army in their midst. New Yorkers began to trust the police, largely thanks to the energy and crime-fighting success of one man, Jacob Hays, the High Constable from 1802 until his retirement in 1844. A short, stocky man of Jewish descent, Hays was known for his fearlessness, strength, and extraordinary ability to bring criminals to justice. During one Fourth of July event in front of City Hall, Hays spotted a wanted criminal in the vast crowd. He handed his staff to an official standing next to him, waded into the throng, grabbed the culprit, and marched him to prison. Hays was famous for his ability to stop a riot without resorting to weapons; he simply knocked the hats off the brawlers and, when they bent to pick them up, pushed them to the ground. This was enough to slow the violence until reinforcements arrived. When Hays shouted, "Now, all good citizens go home!" the rioters knew it was time to disperse. Disobedient children were warned: "Old Hays will be after you!"

Above: A so-called Leatherhead and his sentry box, circa 1825.

Up to this point, New York's police had only rarely worn uniforms. (In 1693, the bellman of the watch had been given a "coat of ye citty livery, with a badge of ye citty arms.") Hays required his watchmen to wear leather hats which resembled a fireman's, only without the front bill; the officers varnished their hats twice a year to keep them as hard as iron. This distinctive headgear quickly earned the force the nickname "Leatherheads." The Leatherheads unfortunately did not equal their leader in zeal and ability, and New Yorkers continued to complain that they were ineffective.

Below: A "Leatherhead" watch helmet, circa 1825.

Between 1820 and 1839, half a million immigrants landed in the Port of New York, and more than a third of them made the city their home for at least a short stay. Many newcomers were Irish and German.

Above: The notorious Five Points District, circa 1830.

Most immigrants from this period were poor peasants and craftsmen who had a difficult time adapting to their new home.

Many settled in New York's growing slums, the worst of which was the notorious Five Points District at the current site of the State and Federal courthouses in Lower Manhattan. Here recent immigrants crowded in dark and pestilential apartment buildings like the infamous Old Brewery, which could barely be called habitable. Without jobs, they turned to prostitution and crime to support their families. If they could not find victims among their neighbors, they ventured out into the surrounding districts to steal what they could. By the 1830s, the Leatherheads would only enter the Five Points in large groups, where they frequently encountered mobs of drunken rioters. Many of these belonged to ethnic gangs like the Forty Thieves, the Plug Uglies, and the Dead Rabbits and were armed with clubs and hobnailed boots. The Board of Aldermen complained:

> Witness the lawless bands of ruffians that stroll about our city, the gamblers, pickpockets, burglars, incendiaries, assassins, and a numerous host of their abettors in crime, that go unwhipt of justice . . .

Above: "Wearing of the Green" sheet music, 1865.

In 1836, a series of strikes and riots prompted politicians to propose forming a large and professional police force to guard the City. Their model was the London police force which had been founded in 1829 by Robert Peel. Conceived as a trained, disciplined, and impartial police force which operated as far as possible from political influence, the so-called Peelers had succeeded in quelling much of the labor and political unrest in industrial London.

New Yorkers wanted a similar organization but remained uneasy about the prospect of a permanent, quasimilitary force in their midst. In 1844, the State Legislature finally authorized the City Council to abolish the Watch Department and organize an 800-man police force. The resolution was nonbinding, however, and Mayor James Harper decided to establish a 200-man Municipal Police force, better known as Harper's Police, over which he exercised great control. Officers were given blue uniforms which many objected to as being an English invention and street toughs said made them look like "liveried lackeys." Harper's party lost the next election, and his successor, William Havemeyer, abolished the Municipal Police and returned to the original idea for an 800-man "Day and Night Police," the direct precursor of today's N.Y.P.D.

Mayor Havemeyer was determined to gain bipartisan support for the new force, so he appointed George W. Matsell of the opposing party as his first Chief of Police. Under Matsell, the police were organized into Patrol Districts divided by wards, each with its own headquarters and Police Court. By August 1845, the first 800 officers were patrolling the city streets. Most were recent Irish immigrants, beginning an Irish-American tradition of police work that continues today. They did not wear uniforms but were identified by the eight-pointed stars (commemorating the eight men of the Rattle-watch) pinned to their street clothes. Nicknamed the "Star" police, the officers followed Matsell's *Rules and Regulations for Day and Night Police,* the precursor of today's police manuals, which delineated duties such as arresting any person driving or riding a horse "through any street, lane, alley or public place within the lamp district, with greater speed than at the rate of five miles an hour." The Day and Night Police gained little public acceptance during its first few years, and some politicians advocated a return to the old watch system.

Above: Portrait of Mayor James Harper.

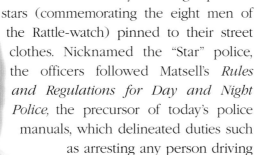

Below: "O'Leary at the Crossing" sheet music.

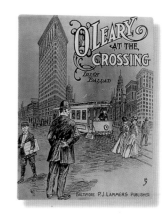

Left: Bust of George W. Matsell, 1875. Matsell was the first Chief (Commissioner) of the New York City Police Department (1845–1857 and 1873–75).

Above: The shield of Captain Galen T. Porter of the 12th Patrol District, circa 1860.

Above: The "police riot" between the Municipal Police (founded in 1845) and the Metropolitan Police (imposed by the state government in 1857). The two forces attacked each other to determine which would police the City. The Metropolitans were the legal winners and became the police force until 1870, when the Municipal Police were reestablished.

Nevertheless the force's efficiency gradually improved, and in 1850, the citizens of Brooklyn adopted a similar system for their community, which by then had grown into a city.

The greatest struggle for the early force was over political control. Too many of the officers, some aged and infirm, were inept cronies of the Aldermen who had the power of appointments for each Ward. In 1853, the City established a Board of Police Commissioners with the sole power to appoint policemen and to fire them (but only with cause). To encourage discipline and earn the public's trust, the Board issued mandatory uniforms consisting of a blue coat with brass buttons, gray trousers, and a blue cap. Officers publicly protested that being forced to buy and wear the uniforms "conflicted with their notions of independence and self-respect"—but the courts upheld the Board's decree. Chief Matsell also instituted the earliest official police training in the form of military drills and gave his men their first standard-issue weapon, a 22-inch wooden club called a "baton."

These reforms were sadly short-lived. In 1854, New Yorkers elected Mayor Fernando Wood, a reformer who abolished the Department's Board of Commissioners, most of whom were appointed by the State Legislature, and placed the force directly under the Mayor's control. Wood claimed this would minimize political interference in police affairs, while his critics accused him of simply furthering his own political ends. In 1857, the State Legislature struck back by voting to abolish the Day and Night Police and establish a "Metropolitan Police" in a district encompassing Manhattan, Brooklyn, Staten Island, the Bronx and Westchester. In response, Wood formed a "Municipal Police," and for two uneasy months the City was patrolled by two rival forces. Officers vied for control of the station houses and even brawled in the streets. The most violent incident occurred when the Metropolitans tried to arrest Wood himself. The Court of Appeals ultimately declared the Municipals unlawful, and Wood's force was disbanded.

At first, the Metropolitan Police were understaffed and ill-equipped to meet the challenges facing them. The day after the

Municipals were disbanded, a small group of Metropolitans were drawn into a deadly riot between the Dead Rabbits (Wood supporters) and the Bowery Boys, avowed enemies of the Mayor. Only the arrival of the National Guard stopped the fighting. Rising crime and mob violence afflicted the city for the rest of 1857, compelling the police board to add new officers. It was not until the Civil War Draft Riots of 1863 that the Metropolitan Police finally earned the respect and admiration of the citizens.

Below: Nineteenth-century Police equipment. Clockwise from top: A gray summer helmet with Roundsman's device, 1885; a "bull's-eye" lantern, circa 1865; a .32 caliber six-shot revolver of the type first issued in the 1870s; an original eight-point shield, circa 1845 (this one is made of brass instead of copper and may have been a supervisor's shield); a "come-along," used to hold onto nonviolent persons; "Lillie" cuffs, circa 1865 to 1870.

Above: Draft rioters in 1863.
Below: Telegraph "sounder," key,
and telegraph rule book for the
Metropolitan Police District
(1857–1870).

THE CIVIL WAR ERA

The outbreak of the Civil War led many of New York's men to enlist for military service. But the war soon took a grimmer course, and by mid-1863 the Confederate Army was threatening Washington, D.C., and reinforcements were needed urgently. The Federal Government began a lottery to draft able-bodied men between 20 and 35 years of age. The only way draftees could avoid service was to pay $300 to hire a substitute. This provision, combined with the high quotas set for New York City, caused much resentment among the working class, whose anger quickly turned to open rebellion. On a hot Monday in July of 1863, thousands of workers began to march north on the main avenues carrying "NO DRAFT" placards. When they arrived at the draft headquarters, they ransacked the building and then burned it to the ground. As soon as the mob spotted Police Superintendent John Kennedy hurrying toward the scene, they seized and beat him. Thus began the most violent series of riots in the City's history.

The police had always relied on the military for reinforcement during outbreaks of mob violence, but now most of the soldiers had been sent south to fight the Confederate Army. The City's 2,000 policemen had only about 300 troops to back them up during the first days of rioting. The burning of the draft office served to whet the appetite of the mob, which now numbered in the tens of thousands. Any reminder of their powerlessness was open to attack—police stations, rich peoples' homes, fancy stores. The first day's most violent fighting took place outside the Mulberry Street police headquarters. The police officials inside realized they had to defeat the advancing mob or the City (and their lives) would be lost. Armed only with their trusty batons, they launched a well-organized counterattack which effectively dispersed the rioters.

The mob soon lost its sense of political purpose but continued to fight for another three days, mainly out of unfocused anger and for plunder. After rioters made repeated attempts to raid the arsenals, the military brought in howitzers to push them back. Tens of thousands of terrified citizens fled the City on ferries and trains. By Friday morning, New York's policemen, many of whom had not slept for days, finally managed to quell the last of the violence. Hundreds of buildings had been burned or ransacked, and historians now believe that over a thousand people were killed. The citizens understood that it was the brave and tireless efforts of the Metropolitan Police that had

Above: During the Civil War considerable unrest occurred in the City as a result of the draft. Many policemen were injured in the course of rioting in July 1863, as illustrated in this vignette from Our Police Protectors, *published in 1883 by Augustine Costello.*

Below: Drilling Metropolitan policemen, circa 1860.

Drilling a Squad of Policemen.

saved the City from total destruction. New York's Governor Seymour later said:

> The draft riots of 1863 were put down mainly by the energy, boldness, and skill of the Police Department.... They proved that the City of New York could, by its police alone, in the absence of military organizations, cope with the most formidable disorders.

In 1872, a committee of leading citizens presented the Department with a flag of honor for "fidelity, discipline, and gallantry" in the Civil War Draft Riots, appending the phrase *Fidelis Ad Mortem* ("faithful unto death"), now the N.Y.P.D.'s official motto.

Below: An 1848 N.Y.P.D. Rules and Regulations book (the first edition was issued in 1845) and an original copper shield vest atop a police blotter (record book) from the same era.

THE GASLIGHT ERA

Control over the Police Department was finally returned to the City government in 1870. This change reflected the phenomenal power that the notorious Boss William Tweed and his Tammany Hall political organization had acquired. Except for a few brief periods of reform government, Tammany ruled New York City well into the twentieth century, exerting a pervasive influence on the practices of the Police Department.

The most notable police officer of the era was Inspector Thomas Byrnes, who was known for his uncanny ability to recover stolen property.

After solving a $3 million bank robbery in the 1870s, Byrnes rose rapidly from patrolman to first Chief of the Detective Squad and finally to Superintendent in 1892. His greatest success was in the Financial District of Lower Manhattan. He told all known criminals that Fulton Street was the so-called Dead Line below which they would be arrested on sight. To insure rapid response, he connected all the major banks to a detective office by telegraph lines. Byrnes cultivated informants throughout the City underworld and could usually return a wallet pick-pocketed from a wealthy businessman within a matter of hours. The brawny detective perfected interrogation techniques using psychology to extract information from suspects. He also opened a room in headquarters for the display of weapons and other artifacts employed in famous crimes and collected photographs of criminals in a Rogue's Gallery that he used for identification purposes.

Mayor William Strong, who took office in 1895, was determined to cleanse the Department of all Tammany Hall influence. He reorganized the Board of Commissioners and appointed a young and enthusiastic Theodore Roosevelt as its head. Roosevelt worked literally night and day to reform the Department. He made physical and mental fitness the prime requirements for new recruits.

Above: Inspector Thomas Byrnes became the first Chief of Detectives in 1882.

Opposite: This painting, used on the cover of Spring 3100, *depicts New York circa 1885.*

Below: Cast-iron Police wagon, circa 1895.

The Heroism of
The NEW YORK POLICE
by Theodore Roosevelt.

In The

OCTOBER
CENTURY

Above: A bicycle cop stops a runaway horse on this magazine cover, circa 1896. Theodore Roosevelt is credited with modernizing and improving the effectiveness of the force as it entered the twentieth century.

He systematized rewards for good police work through medals and promotions and tried to make it easier to dismiss people for incompetent performance. At night, Roosevelt patrolled the streets himself. He also ordered officers to carry a regulation .32 caliber Colt revolver instead of the assemblage of personal firearms they had been carrying. Roosevelt resigned in 1897 to become Assistant Secretary of the Navy. His efforts greatly improved morale and efficiency in the force, not to mention the confidence of the public.

A Tammany-backed candidate won the mayoralty at the end of 1897. This was a crucial election, because on January 1, 1898, the counties of New York, Kings, Queens, the Bronx, and Richmond were consolidated to form New York City, the nation's largest City. Consolidation was crucial for building and connecting the infrastructure that spurred the continued growth of New York into a world center of trade and business.

The N.Y.P.D. made significant steps to better serve the City during this era, becoming a more professional organization with a personnel that more closely reflected the City's ethnic diversity. Matrons had first been hired to look after female prisoners in 1888. In 1918, they were joined by the first group of policewomen. The City's first known African-American officer, Wiley Overton, joined the Brooklyn force in 1891. In 1911, Samuel Battle became the first African-American policeman assigned to

Manhattan, opening the way for men like Wesley Redding, who arrested eight men in one night during his rookie year and in 1920 was named the first African-American detective. His brother George Redding joined the Department in 1927 and rose through the ranks to become a Deputy Chief Inspector in 1959.

Below: (left) An early policewoman brings in the bad guys, circa 1918. The woman shown in this sketch was actually a "Gibson girl" model. (center) A Police Matron, circa 1891. Matrons were appointed to search and transport female prisoners, deal with lost children, and handle other domestic matters. (right) Officer Moses Cobb was one of the first African-American police officers.

Joseph Petrosino and The Black Hand

Italian-Americans began to enter the N.Y.P.D. in the 1880s, and one, Joseph Petrosino, quickly became known for his efficiency and bravery. The Black Hand, the precursor to the Mafia, was then terrorizing merchants in poor neighborhoods like Little Italy and Italian Harlem. Detective Petrosino gained the trust of the community, solved many Black Hand murders, and broke the back of their extortion rackets. In 1905, Petrosino was named head of the elite Italian Mafia Squad, which made thousands of arrests and nearly eradicated the Black Hand.

Above: Lieutenant Joseph Petrosino was assassinated in Sicily while on a fact-finding mission in 1909; he was the first and only N.Y.P.D. officer ever to be killed in the line of duty on foreign soil. Inset: Commemorative button from the funeral of Lieutenant Joseph Petrosino, 1909; ceremonial dagger of the Black Hand, circa 1905; rules and regulations of the N.Y.P.D., circa 1905.

In 1909, while on a secret mission to the Sicilian capital of Palermo, Petrosino was assassinated while standing in a piazza; the killer was probably Mafia leader Don Vito Cascio, whom Petrosino had deported from New York a few years earlier. The Department log noted: "Let his death encourage us all to renewed efforts to stamp out the band of criminals now infesting our city, of which he was a deadly foe." Petrosino's body was returned to New York for a funeral which attracted a quarter of a million mourners.

After writing to you several times you did not even take the trouble to contact us.

Perhaps you think you're dealing with cowards.

In us you find men of heart with blood in our veins and not wretched like yourself. Open your eyes, this is the last letter we are sending you, and if you don't bring the money at the spot we have indicated, you shall pay the penalty with our consecrated dagger that will splash a pint of blood from your heart.

Mind carefully with whom you are dealing. We are not afraid of the poor police. Leave the police in peace and let us earn a living. Don't turn a deaf ear or we will make you a prelate and a doctor of the church.

We don't stand on any sort of ceremonies, nor do we make idle talk.

We give you until Wednesday, at the same place with precise signals at midnight, do you understand?

If you are not punctual to this last assignment you may count yourself among the dead. First you, then your entire family will be riddled through and through.

Furthermore, with our powerful hand we leave no trace and after slaughtering all of you like sheep we use our method with dynamite that makes every bit of flesh disappear.

Advised man is half saved, so if you do not want to buy your death you will bring the money.

We sign ourselves
The Black Hand

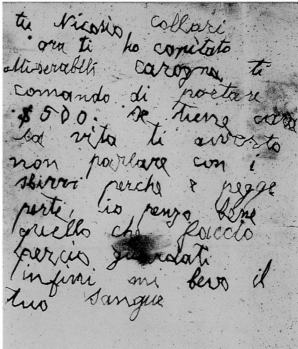

Above: (left) A translation of a Black Hand extortion letter, circa 1908. (right) A ransom letter written in Italian, possibly by a member of the notorious Black Hand, circa 1906.

Above: A "potsey" shield worn by sergeants from 1889 to 1898.

Left: Razors concealed in a hollowed-out book, circa 1880.

Right: Ornate "parade" batons made of carved ivory and hardwood, circa 1885 to 1895. These were sometimes presented to senior officers as retirement gifts from the men of their command.

Left: Three nineteenth-century revolvers. (top) A Colt .45 "Navy" issue, circa 1865; (middle) a Colt .45 six-shot, circa 1870; (bottom) a .32 caliber revolver from the late nineteenth century.

Left: A "day stick" or short baton carried by officers during daylight hours (as opposed to the nightstick), circa 1890.

Below: A nightstick from the late nineteenth century.

Left: Handcuffs and leg irons from the late nineteenth century.

Below: "Palm pistols" like this one were carried by gamblers in the mid-nineteenth century. The barrel protruded between the fingers, and the trigger was pulled by squeezing the hand.

THE N.Y.P.D. TO MID-CENTURY

The Department has always been quick to take advantage of new technologies to make police work more efficient. In 1906, they scrapped the old Bertillon system of criminal classification introduced by Teddy Roosevelt, and replaced it with the fingerprint method that had recently been implemented in England. The old horse-drawn police wagons were replaced by motorized patrol cars, and radios were installed in these beginning in 1917. (The earliest device only transmitted one way and came with a 30-foot antenna attached to the roof of the patrol car). Responding to the increasing complexity of methods needed to combat crime in a vast city, the Department formed specialized units like the Bomb Squad, the Air Service Unit, and the Emergency Services Division. In 1914, police officers created an organization called the Junior Police, which helped the City's disadvantaged youth by involving them in sports like boxing. This program grew into the Police Athletic League (PAL), which offers a wide range of youth programs to more than 60,000 boys and girls each year.

The enactment of the 18th Amendment to the United States Constitution in 1919 inaugurated one of the most frustrating eras in New York City law enforcement: Prohibition. The city's 15,000 pre-Prohibition saloons turned into an estimated 32,000 speakeasies patronized by all levels of society. The bootleggers who supplied the beer and liquor had extensive contacts with the Tammany bosses, and police found that most arrests were voided by Tammany judges and prosecutors. Mobsters like Lucky Luciano and Lepke Buchalter turned from booze to the rackets and soon gained a stranglehold on dozens of industries from prostitution to the sale of kosher chickens. Change finally came in the depths of the Depression. President Franklin Delano Roosevelt won the repeal of

Above: A modern fingerprint equipment case. Fingerprinting techniques originated in England and were introduced to the N.Y.P.D. in 1903.

Opposite: 1920s police officers display their new transport.

Below: The N.Y.P.D.'s first radio-equipped motorcycle, circa 1920.

Above: A Police recruit training class, circa 1912.

Below: The Bomb Squad was created in 1903 under the direction of Lieutenant Joseph Petrosino.

Prohibition in early 1933, and in November of that year Fiorello La Guardia defeated the Tammany candidate in the Mayoral election. One of La Guardia's first hires was Lewis Valentine, better known as the Honest Cop, who became Police Commissioner for a record nine years (1934–1945). Valentine made his philosophy clear during his first few weeks behind the big desk. "Influence, social, political, or otherwise," he told his detectives, "is not going to keep you in the detective division if you are not making good. If you are not making good now, you are on your way out." Valentine's combination of discipline for the force and no mercy for criminals greatly improved the public's confidence in the Department. One by one, the major gangsters were locked up, and the crime rate finally went down after years of increases.

During World War II, thousands of New

York police officers served with distinction in the armed forces, and twenty-four died in service of their country. When peace returned, the City enjoyed about fifteen years of relatively low crime rates. The N.Y.P.D. continued to improve its law enforcement capabilities, taking advantage of technological advances like two-way radios in all patrol cars and perfecting new investigative techniques like ballistic testing and fiber analysis. The first special patrolmen for the subway system were assigned in 1936; in 1953, a separate Transit Police Department was created with 900 officers. In 1952, the patrolmen who guarded the City's housing developments were organized into the Housing Authority Police Department,

(Continued on Page 30)

Above: An officer sorts out a traffic jam on Fifth Avenue in Manhattan, circa 1912. The Traffic Squad was formed circa 1905.

Below: Early communications equipment: desk microphone and intercom control box, circa 1900.

Above: Frankie Yale was a notorious mobster during Prohibition. Yale died in a hail of machine-gun bullets in Brooklyn on July 1, 1927, the first mobster to be murdered by a machine gun in New York City.

Right: This Thompson .45 caliber machine gun with 100-round drum was one of four weapons used in the mobster-style assassination of Frankie Yale in 1927.

Below: Frankie Yale's bullet-ridden body was found beside his crashed car on a Brooklyn street on July 1, 1927.

Frankie Yale loved a good funeral. Born Francesco Ioele, he was an ex-thug from the Five Points Gang who claimed to be a simple Brooklyn undertaker. His real business, however, was bootlegging, and he became the East Coast's largest supplier of illegal liquor. In his spare time, Yale performed contract hits, most notably the murder of Chicago vice boss Big Jim Colosimo. Yale stuck around for the funeral and was awed by the long lines of flower cars and procession of mourners from the political and criminal elite.

In 1928, Yale made a fatal mistake. He started hijacking the trucks filled with bootleg liquor that he was selling to his pal Al Capone in Chicago.

On a warm Sunday afternoon, Frankie Yale took his Lincoln touring car out for a leisurely drive around his south Brooklyn turf. A black Buick pulled alongside, and blasts from a pair of shotguns terminated Frankie Yale. The Lincoln crashed into the stoop of a house where a boy was celebrating his bar mitzvah, and Yale's body fell lifeless onto the sidewalk. "Machine Gun" Jack McGurn pulled out his

THE FRANKIE YALE STORY

favorite weapon and riddled the body for good luck—the first time a machine gun was used in a New York City killing. Four days later, a hundred thousand people jammed the streets to witness the most expensive funeral the city had ever seen.

Above: Frankie Yale was given a lavish mobster funeral in 1927.

Left: A sawed-off double-barrel shotgun concealed in a violin case, circa 1925; the Stetson hat is from the same era.

Below: The science of ballistics involves the use of photographs to compare bullet markings. These samples are circa 1920.

NEW YORK MOBSTERS

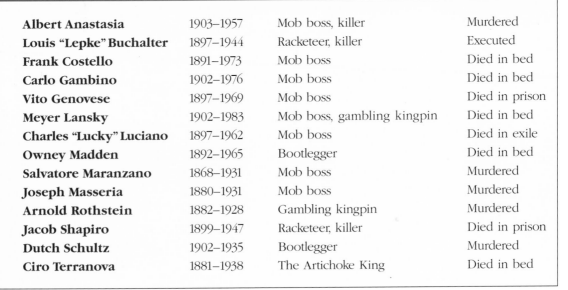

Albert Anastasia	1903–1957	Mob boss, killer	Murdered
Louis "Lepke" Buchalter	1897–1944	Racketeer, killer	Executed
Frank Costello	1891–1973	Mob boss	Died in bed
Carlo Gambino	1902–1976	Mob boss	Died in bed
Vito Genovese	1897–1969	Mob boss	Died in prison
Meyer Lansky	1902–1983	Mob boss, gambling kingpin	Died in bed
Charles "Lucky" Luciano	1897–1962	Mob boss	Died in exile
Owney Madden	1892–1965	Bootlegger	Died in bed
Salvatore Maranzano	1868–1931	Mob boss	Murdered
Joseph Masseria	1880–1931	Mob boss	Murdered
Arnold Rothstein	1882–1928	Gambling kingpin	Murdered
Jacob Shapiro	1899–1947	Racketeer, killer	Died in prison
Dutch Schultz	1902–1935	Bootlegger	Murdered
Ciro Terranova	1881–1938	The Artichoke King	Died in bed

(Continued from Page 27)

Above and below: Front covers of the Department's own publication, Spring 3100, *named after the telephone number of the former police headquarters on Centre Street. The first edition of* Spring 3100 *appeared in 1930, and publication continues to this day.*

which soon became one of the largest police departments in the country. (Both the Transit and Housing Police have since been merged into the N.Y.P.D.) The police emergency phone service was the first in the nation to adopt the 911 system, in 1968; this system was computerized the following year, further reducing police response time to calls from the public for assistance.

From 1960 to 1990, the N.Y.P.D. fought to contain a rising crime rate that was eroding the quality of life in many neighborhoods. Gang violence and a rapidly spreading drug epidemic were the main factors behind this crime explosion. Dozens of police officers sacrificed their lives as the murder rate soared to the highest in the City's history. The widespread use of drugs like heroin and crack cocaine proved particularly difficult to combat. In the mid-1990s, the situation finally began to turn around thanks to new police tactics targeting drug gangs and forging community outreach programs to build police support in neighborhoods devastated by crack and violent crime.

The N.Y.P.D. and its almost 48,000 uniformed officers and civilian workers are now considered one of the most effective police forces in the world. The City's crime rate has fallen steadily since 1990 as New York City has led the way with improved crime-fighting strategies that have been imitated by other cities around the world. Though it is impossible to predict what challenges the future will bring, the N.Y.P.D. continues to build a safer City due largely to the bravery and day-to-day commitment of its officers.

CHRONOLOGY

New Amsterdam in 1664.

1600	
1625	Dutch colonists settle Manhattan Island
1626	Jan Lampo is appointed first law officer
1638	First recorded murder in New Amsterdam
1658	Eight-man Rattle-watch is established
1664	British oust Dutch; city is renamed New York
1700 **1698**	Manhattan population 4,937
1776	Declaration of Independence is signed
1783	Revolutionary War ends in defeat of the British
1789–90	New York is nation's capital, population 33,000
1800 **1802**	Jacob Hays is named High Constable
1820	New York City population 123,000
1844	State Legislature authorizes police force
1845	800-man Day and Night Police, the first N.Y.P.D., is created
1850	New York City population 515,000
1853	Board of Police Commissioners is established
1857	Day and Night force is replaced by state-run Metropolitan Police
1860	Outbreak of Civil War
1870	Control of N.Y.P.D is returned to City
1891	First Police Matrons are hired
1891	First African-American officer is appointed
1894	Lexow Commission investigates corruption
1895–97	Teddy Roosevelt is Police Commissioner
1900 **1898**	Five counties become the five boroughs of New York City
1910	New York City population 4.8 million
1917	First radio is installed in a patrol car
1918	First policewomen are appointed
1919–33	Sale of alcohol is banned by Prohibition
1934	Fiorello La Guardia is elected Mayor
1952	Housing Authority Police Department is created
1953	Transit Police Department is created
1990	New York City population 7.3 million
1995	Housing and Transit Police become part of N.Y.P.D.

Commissioner George W. Matsell's proposed uniform for the N.Y.P.D., nineteenth century.

Title page of Matsell's Rules and Regulations of the Day and Night Police *(1846)— the first "patrol-guide" stating the legal powers and duties of policemen.*

An officer demonstrates how to draw a revolver while while wearing a long coat, circa 1950.

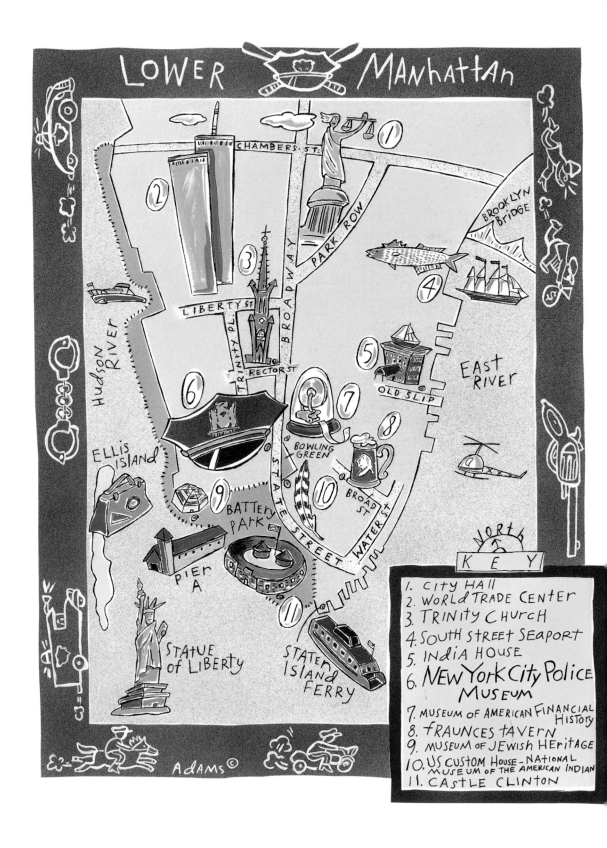

LOWER Manhattan

KEY
1. CITY HALL
2. WORLD TRADE CENTER
3. TRINITY CHURCH
4. SOUTH STREET SEAPORT
5. INDIA HOUSE
6. New York City Police Museum
7. MUSEUM OF AMERICAN FINANCIAL History
8. FRAUNCES TAVERN
9. MUSEUM OF JEWISH HERITAGE
10. US CUSTOM HOUSE - NATIONAL MUSEUM OF THE AMERICAN INDIAN
11. CASTLE CLINTON

THE NEW YORK CITY POLICE MUSEUM

In the heart of Lower Manhattan's Financial District, the New York City Police Museum is one of the city's most exciting and informative tourist attractions. Through interactive displays and hundreds of unique artifacts, the exhibitions in this museum explain the history, duties and challenges of the nation's largest police force. Education is this museum's primary goal, telling the story of the N.Y.P.D. and teaching students about the dangers of drug abuse and youth gangs. The New York City Police Museum is fascinating for adults and children, tourists and police enthusiasts, and active and retired police officers.

The imposing desk that once stood in a police station house greets visitors as they enter the museum. The first exhibition room relates the history of New York City's police force from the landing of the first Dutch colonists all the way up to the present era. Here you can see a display containing dozens of weapons, mug shots of the most famous gangsters and a sawed-off shotgun confiscated from Al Capone. The neighboring exhibit shows what police officers used to fight back, containing standard-issue weapons from the 19th century revolvers to 21st century pistols. Other displays trace the history of police uniforms and badges from the early 19th century "Leatherheads" through today. This history culminates in the COMPSTAT presentation, an audiovisual re-creation of the new strategies used by the N.Y.P.D. to combat crime in every neighborhood of the city.

The next room contains audiovisual displays explaining the activities of some of the N.Y.P.D.'s branches, including the Police Academy and the Housing and Transit Divisions. The videos show the police in action: undercover police officers ride the subway trains looking for criminals; the pickpocket squad arrests thieves whose actions are caught on closed circuit cameras. As part of the museum's anti-drug education program, a display also contains dozens of dangerous drugs and explains their harmful effects.

The story of the N.Y.P.D.'s activities continues in the last exhibition area, a room dominated by an authentic 1972 Plymouth squad car. The display on the Transportation Division also includes vintage motorcycles, a three-wheeled scooter and models of some of the helicopters and airplanes used over the years. Nearby, an exhibit traces the development of police communications from the earliest rattles to radios to today's computers. For amateur sleuths, the museum's most fascinating area is the forensics display. Here you see the scene of a crime, a burglary in an East Village apartment. A detailed chart shows the progress of the investigation from the reporting of the break-in to the arrest of the suspect. The tools of the detective's trade on display include the use of fingerprints and the skills of the police sketch artists. Finally, visitors can take a turn at the Firearms Training Simulator and learn first-hand about the choices faced every day by officers on the streets of the city.

No tour is complete without visiting the museum's gift shop, where visitors can buy caps, t-shirts, mugs, whistles and other souvenirs imprinted with the N.Y.P.D. logo, as well as replicas of police memorabilia, all officially licensed by the N.Y.P.D.

The New York City Police Museum is open daily and is located at **25 Broadway, New York, NY 10004**. Check our website for addiional information at **www.nycpolicemuseum.org**.